SCANDINAVIA

SCANDINAVIA

POEMS

JENN HOWE

LULU PRESS

Title: Scandinavia

Copyright © 2024 by Jenn Howe

All rights reserved.

Except for brief quotations in critical articles
or reviews, no part of this book
may be used or reproduced without the
written consent of the copyright owner.

Printed in the United States of America

First paperback edition: October, 2024

ISBN: 979-8-218-49770-5

Author photo: Jenn Howe

Cover and interior design: Jenn Howe

Book cover and interior files formatted by the author using Adobe InDesign. Cover photo AI generated by combining an original photo by Jenn Howe with the Text to Image (Beta) search terms "solitary candle surrounded by total darkness" in order to create a single, cover-quality image.

Lulu Press, Inc.
Morrisville, North Carolina
www.lulu.com

For Lana Brunelle.

Everything for you.
Anything to break the cycle.

I exist as I am, that is enough.

— Walt Whitman, "Song of Myself" (section 20)

From his collection *Leaves of Grass*, first published in 1855

CONTENTS

~

Read This First — Notes on "Scandinavia"…..xiii

~

PART ONE: FEAR

How Far Away Is Finland?…..3

Child's Play…..6

Delta Kids…..8

Mythological Tales…..9

Marie Antoinette's Head…..10

Your Life, Sober – No Janitor on Duty…..11

Hister, History, Hysteria…..12

I Know Why the Caged Bird Drinks…..13

How to Get Stuck in a Cycle of Loss…..15

32 Questions for a Dead Woman…..16

Upon Hearing Two People Having a Conversation About a Siamese Twin Who Attempted to Sever Herself From Her Other Half…..19

Stockholm Syndrome.....20

Time for a Farewell to Arms.....22

Muse, the M Is Silent.....24

After the Assault.....26

The Unnatural World.....27

Never Been to Norway.....29

The Sounds of Silence.....30

Hyena.....31

Litany.....33

PART TWO: LOVE

Daybreak at the Shoreline.....37

Picking Up the Pieces.....39

Questions About Winter.....40

Once More, with Feeling.....41

Family Ties.....42

The Subconscious Mind Is a Liar.....45

To My Ex-Husband, 23 Years After the Divorce.....46

Welcome to the Sisterhood.....48

The Lesson.....50

He Liked Pretty Things, so He Chose Her.....52

On Incandescence.....53

The Goal.....55

Charger.....56

Something.....59

Watching My Friend Die.....60

Alive.....66

I'm Leaving You for Reykjavík.....67

Nature Documentary Nightmare.....71

Drinking with Ernest Hemingway.....74

Sometimes, Love Is Spelled O-C-D.....76

Reckless Behavior.....78

Pandemic Full Moon.....79

A & W.....81

To My Life Partner.....82

A Bird's View.....84

A World Without Witches.....86

Cheap-Ass, Broke-Down Department Store Houseplant.....89

Social Media, Translated.....92

All the Bikes in Denmark.....93

Scandinavia.....95

The Mighty.....99

From Genesis to Revelation.....102

～

Thank You.....107

About the Author.....111

Read This First — Notes On "Scandinavia"

People often jump to random pages while reading a book of poetry, but **I highly recommend reading the poems of "Scandinavia" in order** — not necessarily all in one sitting (although some people will do exactly that), but from the first poem to the last, as they are presented in the book, with no skips. I assembled these poems in a very specific order, because the overall work represents a trajectory — not just a physical trip from a southern town in the U.S. to a small group of countries in northern Europe, but also the process of moving (mentally and emotionally) from a constant state of FEAR to one of LOVE. This collection is the poetic expression of a person's inner journey as they make their way from surviving trauma and abuse to learning to love themselves and the world around them...to at least some degree, and maybe for the first time.

It doesn't matter if you have five college degrees or if you only completed the fifth grade — "Scandinavia" welcomes you, and **you should be able to understand this book very clearly**. This collection is not pretentious or snobbish, and it doesn't attempt to make you feel ignorant. Simultaneously, it isn't "dumbed down" at all, because I believe in your ability to understand these complex issues and emotions on a very deep level...no matter what formal education you have (or don't have), no matter what income you make, no matter what walk of life you are from. You don't have to feel excluded from the world of poetry...or from any form of art, for that matter. **Art is for everyone**. All people should feel included. **Yes, even you**.

There will always be disagreements about which Nordic countries "officially" belong in the grouping that we call Scandinavia on this planet. **For the purpose of simplification** — and these are the ones I refer to in the book — **we are going to stick with "The Five"** that I learned to be Scandinavia when I attended a World Geography class many moons ago, and they are the following: **Sweden, Norway, Denmark, Iceland, and Finland**.

I'm going to be blunt: **the first section of this book (FEAR) will be difficult to read at times. It deals with dark and painful topics**, including various types of abuse, personal and world-wide violence, and feelings of unworthiness, shame, and hopelessness. These topics are not written about for "shock value" or any kind of self-pity. I wrote about certain horrific events with intention, because millions of people have survived something similar, and I want them to know that a) they are not alone, b) it was NOT their fault and they are not crazy, c) they have a right to speak their truth, and d) not only can they work toward a more functional way of living, but they can also discover healthy, creative, and fulfilling ways to express their own negative feelings and experiences. **If you have not suffered trauma or abuse yourself, this section will still be an important read for you**. It could help you understand why some of your friends, family members, and coworkers act (or react) the way they do in particular situations, and give you a better idea of what they might have lived through. Therefore, I strongly urge all of you, no matter your life experience: **even when it's hard to get through some of the poems in the first half, just as in life...KEEP GOING.** Something positive and uplifting lies ahead.

The second section of this book (LOVE) deals with realizing self-worth, learning to hold yourself in warm regard, discovering and standing in your power, protecting yourself against bullies and abusers, and the magic and beauty of life on Earth...because no matter what happens, there is always something miraculous to behold and appreciate on this planet. **The back half of "Scandinavia" is designed to be entertaining, varied, and — most of all — inspiring**. It contains poems about a termite invasion, a philosophical housecat, a dying plant I saved from a department store, obsessive-compulsive disorder (and the offbeat way my daughter chooses to deal with it), a conversation I had one night with a famous dead writer, and my anxiety over accidentally killing a gnat. **There are bittersweet moments, humorous tales, and universal truths. In short, there should be something for everyone**.

I spent many years in therapy and counseling, healing myself after decades of trauma and abuse. Today, as I write these last few words of the book and prepare it for print, I'm more balanced and functional than I ever thought would be possible, and I love my life very much — whether or not I have a car, a dream job, a ton of money, a romantic partner, or anything else. Now, I don't rely on any person, situation, or thing to provide my sense of self or my "happiness" —

true contentment can only come from within. Now, I know that I have inherent worth, and I truly respect and value myself, setting boundaries and not allowing anyone to mistreat me. Now, I live authentically and I stand in my own power. **It is my sincere hope that you, Reader, can experience a similar trajectory in your life — that you can find and follow a path that will lead to you becoming your most functional, authentic, content, and empowered self.**

But first, I hope you will make THIS voyage — through the poems of this book, through the unlimited space and time available in your mind, and through the endless rooms of love, compassion, and resilience that exist inside the human heart. And so, without further ado, I invite you to find a peaceful and comfortable spot where you won't be disturbed. Light a candle and sit for a few moments in silence, then turn to the first page and come with me on the journey through "Scandinavia" …

Your poetry mom,
Jenn Howe

August 26, 2024

PART ONE

FEAR

How Far Away Is Finland?

How did I get here?
I ask the spider on the ceiling
as I lie in a bathtub
full of partially rusted water.
At least the pipes still work,
but the ticking of the clock
is like the timer on a bomb:
the 25-year-old car stopped working,
the bank account has 14 dollars in it,
the roof is caving in.
Even the roaches inside the walls
click their crunchy legs
in a constant state of anxiety.
They depend on me.
Everything depends on me.

I tried my best
I tell the inhabitants of the house.
The cats are perched on the countertop.
They watch me as I watch the spider,
and she watches over the silken sac
that protects her unborn babies.
I can't make them understand that
the universe doesn't always reward
the diligent or the kind.
It doesn't matter that I work until I bleed
and always try to do what's right.
My entire existence is duct-taped together.
The seams are bursting and
new leaks sprout every day.

I love you
I say to everyone and no one.
There is no significant other.
No willing ears to catch my troubled thoughts,
no words of understanding or sincerity,
no gentleness for my heart to nestle in.
I sleep with my own arm tucked around my body.
There is no "emergency contact,"
whether I'm filling out paperwork
or crawling from the wreckage of a car crash,
and I can't fathom the luxury of performing
only half of life's heavy lifting.

What would that even feel like?
I whisper into the rising steam.
I recently paid plastic money
just to feel another person touch me
in a way that wasn't callous or unbidden,
and I cried on the masseuse's table
because the feeling was so foreign.
I have only known a revolving door of bad men
with porn-infested minds, cold hearts, and greedy hands.
Men who live only to lie, degrade, and objectify.
Men who are just like the roaches —
they always come running
when something sweet but damaged
is left out in the open, unprotected.

5,016 miles
I announce to the bathroom crowd.
That's the distance from this decaying house

to Helsinki, the capital of Finland.
It is one of several Nordic places
I hope to see before I die,
but it feels as far away
as every dream I've ever had.
The tragedy is this:
I'm only one of millions who were
violated or abused and left to believe
that dreams are not for them.
I'm only one of millions who were
made to feel like a stain on this planet,
something that should be scrubbed away.
I'm only one of millions who were
handed a heavy bag full of broken pieces
and told to go build a life.
We are the shell-shocked army of We Can't,
We Shouldn't, and We Don't Deserve.
We can only fight to find meaning
as we stumble into the future with a shattered compass,
thousands of miles from feeling worthy or good enough.

Will I ever get there?
I moan to the universe,
and a piece of plaster falls from the ceiling.
We all stop moving —
human, cats, spiders, and roaches —
this growing family of several thousand,
all of us holding our breath and sitting in silent horror
as we wait to see what will happen next
and whether or not I'll recover.

Child's Play

I was a seven-year-old girl with a free Sunday morning,
and I sat on the couch beating my doll.
She'd done nothing wrong, but that didn't matter
when playing this particular game.
I hit her because I'd learned from experience:
that's what you do when you care about someone.
I'd been bowled over by such affection myself,
and had watched the bruises on my body change color
with horrific fascination — putrid purple,
gut-churning green, approach-with-caution yellow.
My toddler brother was also showered with adoration.
He would roll himself into a self-protective sphere,
only to become a frantic human soccer ball
that begs and shrieks as it's kicked around the trailer.

There were so many demonstrations of endearment in our family.
Prisoners of love, held captive inside our home,
we'd scream and swoon from room to room
as the blood and tears rained down,
police officers shouting at the door,
a crowd of curious neighbors growing outside.

On this particular Sunday,
I was punching my doll's small, plastic face
when I glanced up to find you standing in the doorway.
You were watching me and making a face of disgust,
as though you'd never seen anything so hideous.
After a moment of silence,
you shook your head and said, "You're so stupid,"
then you left the room and I was forced
to sit alone, feeling like a bag of garbage.
But I couldn't understand why I felt so embarrassed.

After all, I was only trying to be just like you.

Even the strongest little girl has a breaking point.
On that day, the hopeful part of me gave up —
it just stood up and walked out on me forever.
My babyish and gullible origami mind folded in on itself
as it tried to make a sensible shape of the madness,
but I only found two things to be certain:
nothing in this world is safe,
and there must be something wrong with me.

I returned to my game, but now the rules were different.
From that day forward, the doll would always be me.
I looked into her expressionless eyes and hissed,
"You are so stupid."
Then I drew my arm back as far as it would go,
because I wanted to hit her with all my might —
hard enough to make her stop feeling,
so hard she would cease to exist.

Delta Kids

In the distance, the sky lies stick-straight
on this flat mattress of earth
that stretches all the way to the muddy Mississippi.
The only richness that exists around here
is in the ground beneath our grubby bare feet,
in the dirt that nurtures the soybeans that grow behind our trailer.
At twilight, we listen to the locusts scream as we stare into the fields.

Hopelessness and shame are what we have inherited.
This part of the world was built upon
the strong backs of mistreated people.
Their sweat and tears seeped into the soil.
The crops were harvested and the children ate the sadness.
That's how we got The Blues,
which isn't merely a sound, but the wailing of the soul.

Now, these are fields of chemicals and machines.
It is the crop duster, not the dove, that flies overhead.
The large metal birds swoop down low and
drop the poison that protects the plants,
but who will protect us
from pesticides or the sins of our fathers?

And this is my confession: I am the one who made the crop circles.
I'd been attempting to outrun
other things that grow abundantly here —
hatred and intolerance, addiction and abuse, poverty and apathy.
Time and again, I ran with all my might
only to end up right back where I'd started.
Thus began my endless spiral. So much frantic spinning,
searching for any path to a life without limits,
wondering how to escape without dying or going over the edge
in this place where the Earth remains flat.

Mythological Tales

When you glance up at the night sky
and see the slight, white-silver
sliver of a crescent moon,
it means that God
is clipping his fingernails.

When you hear the booming rumble
of thunder during a storm,
it means that God
is enjoying a game of bowling,
and He just rolled a strike.

When slick, torrential sheets of rain
slide down from the heavens,
it means that God
is taking a shower,
cleansing himself and the earth below.

When a child is made to feel
unlovable, unworthy, and unwanted —
when a part of their heart dies forever,
leaving them to shrivel in despair
and shriek into empty rooms or uncaring faces —
what does *that* mean?
Where is God during those moments,
and what in the world could He be doing then?

Marie Antoinette's Head

Facedown and strapped to a deathbed plank,
she waited for the blade to drop.
She was cleanly clipped
and the tip of her body tumbled.
Not head over heels, but forehead over chin —
one small somersault, both grisly and graceful.
Her flying eyes were swiftly filled with
steel, scaffold, sky, spectators,
then darkness as the thinking part of her
thumped into a wicker basket.
Since the brain is a squishy-yet-steadfast computer
that fights to keep running no matter the damage,
she was still painfully aware
when someone grabbed a fistful of her badly shorn hair
and lifted her lid back into chaotic brightness.
Dangled up high and forced to look at the crowd,
she saw not only a sea of ravenous people,
but all of mankind in the centuries yet to come.
As blood and consciousness drained from her head,
the last queen of France was ready to be dead.
She didn't wish to hang around
and see what humans would do next,
for she knew without doubt there would be no end
to men using violence to control other men.

Your Life, Sober — No Janitor on Duty

When the good times stop rolling
and the spirits stop flowing
and your pills and needles stop showing
(should that day arrive),
you'll come to in a room scattered with
the remnants of miracles and answered prayers,
each one dismissed and discarded,
shattered to bits on the dusty floor —
the monumental waste of the
self-centered and careless.

You had it all, you know?
And should you awaken too late,
the only sound you'll hear
in that littered solitude of your own making
will be the echoing footsteps
of the few people who truly cared
as they head for the nearest exit door.
Even the most devoted caretakers reach a point
where they can't — and won't — clean up
your self-inflicted messes anymore.

Hister, History, Hysteria

"Beasts ferocious with hunger will cross the rivers. The greater part of the battlefield will be against Hister. Into a cage of iron will the great one be drawn, when the child of Germany observes nothing." – Nostradamus, 1555

Has humankind learned nothing?
In school, the facts of
the Third Reich were drilled into us.
One cannot shake it,
the terror of that time when the
mark of a madman was held high
and heels clicked in time
to the rhythm of death's drum.
A mass of puppeteered people
was programmed to smite
the so-called subhuman ones.
This catastrophic coma of many
ended only with a wound to the head.
But horror and murder
have never been limited to camps,
and there is always a new tune
with a similar refrain of divide and conquer.
To bomb any part of this planet
is to burn down your own house.
To trample on the rights or bones of any human
is the boot in the face of your own mother.
Why do I see armies of people
still marching in the opposite direction of progress?
Compassion is the great lesson
that man has not mastered.
Like any nightmare,
these ongoing atrocities could end
before reaching a sickening conclusion,
yet so many choose to remain in the dark,
preferring the oblivion of sleep.

I Know Why the Caged Bird Drinks

Because she could only mimic what was
modeled in her environment, as parrots do.

Because in her environment,
there was always an open bar.

Because this is her normal.
She has only ever known
the beer can in someone's hand,
the wine-stained shirt, the whiskey breath,
the harsh words, the fear, the fist.

Because alcohol temporarily makes her
forget that she isn't loved,
or else it leads her to do intimate things
with people who do not love her,
but sometimes those things feel a bit like love —
albeit not the kind of love she needs.

Because drinking feels like the only way
to escape the hell that surrounds her
without actually escaping.

Because the few times she did manage to escape,
she crashed down and crawled right back into
one type of confinement or another —
a toxic friend group, an abusive relationship,
and once, after being arrested, a jail cell —
because one becomes institutionalized,
and a cage is a cage is a cage.

Because in her world, freedom from pain
doesn't exist, not even in song.
Instead of singing, she screams, or cries,
or — most often — makes no sound at all.
And yes, she drinks.

Because I used to be her.

And I'd tell her that others may have
clipped her wings, broken her spirit,
and removed the tiny mirror from her cage
so she couldn't see the truth of who she is,
but if she would just turn around
and really look at the dirty window behind her —
not at the grime and muck standing between
herself and a world of possibilities,
but at her own reflection, barely visible —
she might faintly see it for the first time:

That she is a dazzling, unique, and majestic being.
That she was built not only to be powerful and free,
but to soar to heights she never thought possible.
That everything she was made to believe about herself
has been lies, all lies, nothing but lies.

How to Get Stuck in a Cycle of Loss

Loss of nerve.
Words not spoken,
action not taken.
The great chance, missed.

Unyielding pain.
A mountain of shame.
Aborted plans and
a life of limits.

No growth or self-reflection.
The spark of desire and
a new opportunity.
Loss of nerve.

32 Questions for a Dead Woman

Written while sitting at the tombstone of Eliza G. Randall, who lived and died on Star Island (seven miles off the coast of New Hampshire) in the 1800's

Did they call you "Liza" for short?
Were you petite and delicate, or large and powerful?
Did you consider yourself pretty?
Was physical beauty of any importance to you?

Did you love yourself?

Were you brazen, or were you timid and fearful,
white-knuckling it all the way to the grave?

What were your passions or hobbies?
Did you have time for them?

Were you a good cook?
Did you loathe this never-ending, female-appointed task,
or did you take delight in it?

The rocky refuge you called home
is now a place of retreat for most,
but what was it for you?
Was it endless years of fish and tide and harvest,
fetching and lifting and scrubbing,
mending by candlelight?

Were you forced to endure the difficult labor
of both man and woman,
without anesthetic or reprieve?

Did you love the island, or were you a city girl
trapped in a water-locked hell?
Was the sound of seagulls pleasing to you,
or did their calls make you shiver as though

they were icy winds from the North Atlantic?

Were you grateful to turn 40?
After all, in your day,
wasn't 40 the new 90?

Did you wish to marry your husband,
or did your parents auction you off like a farm animal,
as was commonly the custom?

Did you curse your lot as a woman?
Were you treated solely as a penis repository
and baby-making machine?
Did anyone make you feel
that you had value or worthwhile opinions?

With your rib cage clutched in a whalebone grip,
did you want to submit?
Or did your binding make you want to fight?

Would you believe that millions of women are still fighting?

Did you enjoy your life?
Would you do it all again,
or would you take a pass on a second chance?

Did you see death coming?
Was it easy, or did you struggle
in an attempt to stay tethered
to your temple of skin and bone?

What is it all leading to?

Can you see me now from somewhere
in the eternal ether that others imagine?
Or did you fade away, with your last breath,
into peaceful forever nothingness?
Were you simply — like a candle's flame — extinguished?...
Flicker, poof, and gone.

Upon Hearing Two People Having a Conversation About a Siamese Twin Who Attempted to Sever Herself From Her Other Half

I found myself straining to figure out
what misunderstanding or calamity
could cause a person
to attempt such a violent separation,
to reach for the nearest knife or hacksaw.

Could they not reach an agreement?
Was the one on the right a Republican
and the left one a Democrat?
Did one sister dream of a cottage
on the rocky coast of Maine
while the other wished to set up camp
in the wide-open west?

Did one of them turn her head
(already so close to the other's ear)
and whisper, *I know you are, but what am I?* —
and it was just the one time too many,
the last straw,
the one that broke the bones
in the back they shared?

Or maybe, it was the simple truth
that being in the constant company
of the wrong person
feels more lonely than being alone,
more terrifying than the risk of freedom.

Stockholm Syndrome

As a child,

I learned to deny my true feelings
and fake a laugh or force a smile
so I wouldn't be shamed for crying
or being *too sensitive*.

I learned to choke on my fear
and stay silent or say yes
when all that was holy in the universe
demanded a resounding *NO*.

I learned to act as though I agreed
when I actually had a differing opinion,
just to avoid being ridiculed
for simply being myself.

I learned to cower and crouch and hide
and not look people in the eyes,
because I could not value myself as
a worthy or precious human being.

I learned to believe that violent acts
and unkind words must equal
Love, so much Love,
since these things were clearly allowed
and accepted on a regular basis
in my mangled world.

I learned to always pretend that everything is fine,
even after watching something horrific
unfold right in front of my face,

for one must keep the offender happy
and their sins hidden, at all costs.

But this, Reader, is MY sin:

as a result of my distorted education
in trauma and dysfunction,
each time I dated a man who
insulted, degraded, or abused me,
I did something even worse —
I let them.

Time for a Farewell to Arms

Just look at that red, white, and blue!
It's the land of the free, the home of the brave.
We've no need to worry and we'll always be safe.
We'll protect ourselves with our guns.

Just look at that red, white, and blue!
Stolen from the native and built by the slave —
this land that wasn't ours, we decided to take
with the cunning use of guns.

Just look at that red, white, and blue!
We police the world, we're here to save the day.
And you know what makes our country so great?
Well of course, it's the strength of our guns.

Just look at that red, white, and blue!
These colors don't run! And there's nowhere we can run
because the danger was right here all along —
we're destroying ourselves with our guns.

Children are being slaughtered, dropping like flies.
It's so commonplace we're no longer surprised,
but too many people just want to be right
and fight to keep all the guns.

But everything will be okay — just keep chanting to yourself:
Our guns will keep us safe
Our guns will keep us safe
Our guns will keep us safe
Our guns will keep us safe
Our guns will keep us safe

American life is now like a horror film,
and here comes the plot twist...
Hey, babysitter – the murderer is calling you
from a phone inside the house.
Hey, trapped cave explorer – you've awakened only to realize
that your escape was just a dream.
Hey, innocent school kid – you're about to be gunned down
in your seventh period science class.
Hey, countrymen – the terrorist is an American.

Just look at that red, white, and blue.
Land of the frightened, our home a mass grave.
What will you do when the grieving parent is you?
Will you tuck your weapons into bed at night?
Will you kiss and hold your guns?

Will you continue to ignore the rivers of gore
that stain our school yards, churches, and stores?
Everywhere, the blood of the slain —
on hands that take money from the NRA,
but on yours, too, if you don't cry out for change.

Just look at that — no, don't turn your head.
Make yourself see it and forget your foolish pride.
This terror has to end, there are too many dead.
It's time for you to wake up and
just look at all...that...red.

Muse, the M Is Silent

So, you have become a muse.
Aren't you such a lucky girl,
to be admired for everything that you are not?
All will be well, as long as you remember
that the first letter in that word
should be silent: *use*.

And you will be used —
prepared and primped,
(or is it pimped?)
photographed, painted,
and made into a fantasy.
That is all they want, not anything real.
You must hold up the illusion at all costs,
do your best come hither, bat your eyes,
be what they desire.

They certainly won't tolerate anything authentic,
like the deepening lines on your face
or an opinion.
Not for long, anyway.
You are only of interest for a limited time,
until you are no longer the new and sparkly
plaything in the toy box.
Once they realize they can't have sex with you,
or after they do and then quickly tire of you,
or when you've reached some
arbitrary and imaginary expiration date,
you are simply thrown away.

Had Marilyn survived that overdose,
she soon would have been even more disappointed,

for in time, she too would have been discarded,
deemed as unnecessary as that letter M in muse.

The art you inspire will survive both
the cruel dismissal and the years to come...
but will your heart?

After the Assault

"Pics or it didn't happen,"
said the man who believes in God.

The Unnatural World

"People in the final stages of hypothermia engage in 'paradoxical undressing' because, as they lose rationality and their nerves are damaged, they feel incredibly, irrationally hot." – online article, by Esther Inglis-Arkell. Published on gizmodo.com on February 26, 2015.

Just try to imagine it:
suddenly feeling warm in the final moments
before you freeze to death —
so much so that you begin stripping off your clothes,
exposing your blue extremities directly to the
snow and biting wind that is killing you,
helping death along.

It might seem impossible,
but unbelievable things happen every day.
A person at rest in a chair
can spontaneously burst into flames,
an amputee can feel physical pain in a leg
that was severed and discarded years before,
and some parents murder their own children
and bury their bodies in the basement.
If we wanted a world that makes sense,
we certainly came to the wrong planet.

This is the unnatural world,
where I spent too much time striving and starving
for the affection of the one person
who should most freely give it,
leaning into the cold shoulder
of someone incapable of love.

And I had so much in common with
a plane crash survivor who is
stranded and stripped nude
on the side of a remote, icy mountain —

both of us victims of temporary and misleading warmth, waiting for the breakthrough that would never happen, believing that things might turn around for the better when really, it was the beginning of the end.

Never Been to Norway

I've never been to Norway
or stood in Arctic snow,
but I have known the anguish
of a life spent in the cold.

I've not been in an avalanche
or slipped through cracking ice,
but I have felt a biting chill
that kills you from inside.

And when it comes to frigid fates,
there is no worse demise
than to face a boundless blizzard
of brutality and slight.

No colder execution
could be ordered from above
than to slowly freeze a heart to death
by withholding the warmth of love.

The Sounds of Silence

The absence of sound is not silence.

Inside the perfect vacuum of a tightly sealed room,
one can still perceive a slight, high-pitched ringing.

Enveloped in the hush of a monastery,
the monk must tame the relentless chatter
heard within the mind's ear.

The family pet will respond to a dog whistle,
though its shriek passes through
human senses undetected.

Everything in the universe emits a frequency,
regardless of one's ability to be aware.

But what of the acoustics of emotion,
the vibrations of sentiments and desires?

As I place a palm over my heart
and ponder the message that
it sends out on invisible waves,
a deaf woman, long buried in a nearby cemetery,
twists in her tomb —
just enough to free her arm, lift a bony hand,
and sign the word
desolation.

Hyena

And you thought giggling in church was bad.

I once laughed out loud as I witnessed
the vicious beating of someone I love —
but it wasn't quite as simple as that.
I'd been made to watch a display
of such violence and hate
that my sanity suddenly cracked.
My mind overloaded and my prepubescent form
switched to a sick type of autopilot,
forcing my body to commit this incongruous act.
My system was in shock — a state
I couldn't control, much less understand —
but the person being beaten
was not comforted by this fact.

That was the moment when a giant —
a gogmagog of inappropriate response —
sat on my chest and swallowed an anchor,
deciding to stay forever. And every day
since has been Opposite Day.
I'm an endless stream of giggles and guffaws
when I'm anxious, nervous, or scared.
I cry when I feel true happiness or safety,
because their occurrence in my life is so rare.
I'm a creeping galaxy of awkwardness,
unable to maintain eye contact
or properly convey how much I care.
Just a blushing, bumbling, stuttering mess,
cursed to always cause discomfort,
stung and shamed by all the confused stares.

Run away from me.

I'm telling you: I'm *still* cracking up.
Not fit to be with other humans,
I'm broken beyond repair.
I may not be guilty, but cast me out.
Send me away to some subdesert or savanna
and leave me to what I always knew would be my fate —
to roam in darkness with the
other misunderstood and cackling creatures,
lost, bound for no place but hell,
laughing all the way.

Litany

Hail Mary, full of grace,
the Lord is with thee.
(But is He with us?)
Pray for those who were defenseless and abused.
(Now and at the hour of our next panic attack.)

Pray for the innocent who were brutally broken.
(For we were cursed instead of blessed.)
Our only sin was to believe we'd be cared for.
(Oh, the mystery of faith.)

The dangerous ones are not always strangers.
(They were locked inside the house with us.)
We needed protection.
(Pray for us.)
We who were preyed upon.
(Pray for us.)
We lifted our hearts.
(And they were crushed.)
We were made to feel worthless.
(How is this just?)

Was this His will, done on Earth?
(Please, ask Him to graciously hear us.)
Surely each one of us is more than a prisoner,
a piece of property, or a punching bag.
(Will He ever have mercy on us?)

May we forgive those who trespassed against us.
(Please heal our traumatized hearts.)
May we love and be loved in return.
(Without being torn apart.)

May we be relieved of this anchor of shame.
(The unfair load we've been forced to carry.)

For our bodies, hearts, and minds should have been safe and revered by all, for ever and ever...

PART TWO

LOVE

Daybreak at the Shoreline

I crawled to get here.
I am kneeling at the edge of everything,
at the place where the land meets the sea.
Is it a beginning, or a finale?
Perhaps this is intermission.

The great, black curtain is down.
The theatre is dark, save for the lamps
that sparkle light years above,
as distant as my understanding of things.
Do I dare to make a wish?

It has been the longest night —
so many tragic years laid end to end.
But what if each brutal or blistering experience
had a purpose yet to be revealed to me?
What if the pain was a preparation
and a call to rise above?
I wait here, in stillness.

The glittering backdrop fades as that
spectacular burning spotlight rises center stage.
Birds, sand, waves, and stones
emerge from the shrinking darkness
slowly, like timid thespians.
But in the manner of the most experienced players,
they speak volumes without saying a word,
and their message is absolute:

*If you are able to witness all of us,
then you are meant to be here, too —*

all things exist for a reason.
You are integral to the meaningful plot of the universe,
with your own unique and important part to play.
Lean into your role, before it's too late.
Accept your gifts. Step into your power.
It's time.

Picking Up the Pieces

The sea slams onto the land
and drops the tiny treasures
upon the wet, hard-packed sand.
I eagerly stoop to scoop them up,
these bleached and colorful riches
that have escaped the roaring giant's
blue-green, liquid clutches.
I gather as many as I can fit
into my fist, then listen to the
click and clatter as I drop them
into the net that's resting on my hip.
Some think it's strange to harvest
the scuffed and battered armor of
gummy mollusks now departed.

They've all been tossed
and tumbled by life's tides,
so most of them are only fragments —
just coastal debris in many people's eyes.
I pick up the scattered pieces
to examine their splendor
and adore them simply for what they are,
each one perfectly imperfect
with their cracks, missing parts, and scars.
If a greater being were to pick me up,
would I be viewed in the same manner?
Can I be this badly broken
and still be worthy of such admiration?
Could I ever have that type of grace
or mercy for my own being —
to view myself with true appreciation,
to hold myself inside that kind of love?

Questions About Winter

What if the occasional
biting pain and bitter chill
are necessary components of growth?
What if migratory birds
are here to teach us to
periodically change our perspective,
because remaining stagnant
leads to a slow and certain death?
What if we chose to discard
all that is negative or unnecessary,
the way deciduous trees
drop their leaves and soften their form
so that the cold does not break them?
What if we turned inward
and made peace with our shadows,
settling into the darkness like
the snake, the woodchuck, and the bear?
What if the planet
is only asking you to rest?
What if we welcomed the winter
as nature's long night —
the great sleep
which would allow us all
to dream our greatest dreams,
then emerge refreshed and renewed,
ready to bring them into being?

Once More, with Feeling

The twelve months of another time table,
ticked off seemingly faster
than the twelve before.
More lines for my face,
tiger stripes of courage and experience.
What is this battle-scar bravery good for?
I feel the self-splitting ache
of the outer shell decaying
as the mind ripens and grows more seductive.

So much exhausting, overtime analyzation...
What should I do? What does it all mean?
I can't find the means to an end I can't see.
This giant rock we're riding on
is flying 67,000 miles per hour
and narrowly avoiding space trash
as I wastefully rummage for reasons why.
One day soon, Earth will do its
celestial spin-top dance without me,
and my questions will be put to a stop,
with or without my understanding.

I am left with only this:
I'm still a participant, and it's now.
I strike through the date on the calendar
and prepare myself for another
mystical trip around the sun —
once more, with feeling.

Family Ties

They're hateful and dangerous.
They keep me sick and miserable.
But I'm related to them, so I can only
deal with it and suffer in silence.

Not all ties that bind are holy.
You don't owe anyone a relationship
just because they spread their legs or their seed
and brought you into this world,
or because you share the same
eye color, surname, or blood type.

But they're my family member,
and you know what they say:
family comes first, always.

Lizzie Borden was a sister,
Andrea Yates was a mother,
Ted Bundy was someone's son,
and The Green River Killer was a father,
so what's your point?

The word family *can* mean:
a genetic connection, or close relations
through marriage or other circumstances.
What the word family is *not* guaranteed to mean:
supportive, caring, rational, or even safe.

And an act of murder isn't the only way
that a person can steal someone else's life.

But you can never turn your back on your kin.

Oh yes, you can. You are allowed
to walk away from a toxic family tormentor,
and if they scream at you and call you
Ungrateful or Unloving or Bitch,
remember that you are none of these things,
and know that their anger is not righteous —
it is only a boulder of guilt
they are trying to pass over to you
because they can't bear its weight,
but it is not yours to carry.
Let them hold it.
Let them sink to the bottom
of their lake of denial with it,
and stop trying to save them
from themselves, because you can't.

But if I cut them off,
what will everyone say?

Who cares. You don't have to remain
DNA-chained to your kindred abuser.
Don't let society senselessly shame you into
a lifetime of dysfunction and misery just because
that has always been the widely-accepted way.

But blood is thicker than water!
Blood is, blood is...

just blood.
Cut the cord and let the connection bleed.
Let it all bleed out, and leave the scene
of all the crimes that you never committed.

Run away, fast and screaming for help if you must.
Ring all the bells and sound all the alarms
as you finally make your way
to a place of assistance and
the protection you have always deserved.
You have a need to be safe,
you have a right to be free,
and sometimes,
the only person you can save —
and should save —
is yourself.

The Subconscious Mind Is a Liar

The trauma-related tape-on-repeat
that plays in your head once served you well.
Perhaps it even saved your life, but now
those outdated beliefs won't work.

A healthy, balanced, and functional existence
is something even you deserve,
so let me debunk some dangerous myths,
because you weren't made to always hurt:

You don't have to be a martyr in order to matter.
You don't have to expect and accept only the worst.
You don't have to feel guilty for someone else's sins
or pretend to be okay when you are deeply disturbed.
You don't have to always be the winner to be loveable.
You have a right to be loved as you are,
even if you've never come in first.
You don't need to do tricks and flips
to garner respect or be impressive.
You have nothing to prove during your time on Earth.
You don't have to torture yourself by striving to be perfect,
trying to force what's impossible
in an effort to earn your value or your worth;

those two things are yours already.
And despite all the lies
someone programmed into your mind,
you've had them since the day of your birth.

To My Ex-Husband, 23 Years After the Divorce

You became the prisoner of a war
you knew nothing about,
without even being an enemy.

When you first met me,
I was fresh from the horror —
shell-shocked and stunted,
terrified of everything,
raging against myself and the world.

You had only wanted
to build a life with me,
but how could you live in peace
with a person who was born
into chaos and violence?
You handed me normalcy
and I didn't know what to do with it.
Where were the cruel comments?
The slaps and screams?
The familiar hammer blow to my heart?
I kept re-living old traumas
and creating new dramas,
because that was all I knew.

Doomed to fail, you fought anyway.
You fought for me and tried to save us.
You deserved so much better.

There should be a Medal of Honor
for those who must deal with
a member of The Broken
when they were not the one

responsible for breaking them.

We weren't meant to stay married,
but after decades of healing myself,
I can finally see you for what you really are,
and I offer my sincere apology
and deepest respect to *you* —
patient warrior, tireless protector,
co-creator, ally,
hero.

Welcome to the Sisterhood

My daughter has a broken heart
and I cannot rest.
I watch over her sleeping body
like a mother wolf bent over her pup,
snarling, howling into the night,
prepared to kill in order to protect.

But she has already been rocked
by the great pain that I can't prevent.
The stinging shock of deception has
caused a seismic shift inside her,
and the emotional landscape
will never be the same.
Her step will now be hesitant and unsteady,
her future decisions darkened by doubt.

I am powerless, just as I was when
she had the flu as an infant
and I could only bear witness to her terror.
Crying in a cold, clinical room and
catching her vomit in my hand,
I tried to explain to this tiny person
who did not yet have a language:
If you can just ride out the storm,
you will laugh and play again.
Each hard-won battle
will leave you with a new immunity
and a renewed lust for life.
You must fight, little one,
and always keep a hopeful heart.

Now, I wait for her to awaken

so we can begin the ritual.
I will light candles and
bring her comfort foods
dense with sugar and carbs.
We will watch comedies
in an effort to laugh and forget,
even if just for a moment.
She will remember and be rattled
again and again, until she prays for amnesia.
She will ask questions
and I will respond truthfully:
No, you are not overreacting.
Yes, you are more than enough —
never forget how special you are.
No, I don't know why people do these things.
Yes, you will survive this.

Mostly, I will be silent
as she spills her pain repeatedly
and tries to make sense of it.
I will listen as she tells
her own version of the familiar story —
the one I recited each time
I was the one whose heart was broken,
as we all have been or will be.
But there is safety and solace in the sisterhood,
where each generation of females
comforts the next as best they can
in this daisy chain of pain and recovery
that reaches both backward and forward,
unbroken, into forever.

The Lesson

I lie in bed and watch my gray tabby
as she sits in an open window
taking in the universe.
My euphoric little feline is high on life
as her eyes devour all things
that are laid before her.

Her head swivels toward
the snap of a cracking twig
and she waits, on high alert,
in case it has anything further to report.
Several birds fly by, and it's An Event —
an air show just for her entertainment.
A leaf falls from a high branch,
and she watches it descend with the concentration
of a person performing CPR,
a life hanging in the balance.
The nostrils of her rubber eraser nose
flare and shrink as she savors each scent
that floats on the wind.
She makes the chirping and chuffing noises
of a blissed-out creature,
then slowly tilts her head backward
and lifts her furry face to the sun in appreciation.
Her contentment is total.

Her simple mind is not a deficit,
but the very thing that saves her
from the misery of a wasted life.
What is there to worry about?
She can't remember.
It's as though that dreadful day

at the vet's office never happened,
and no future problems can exist
in a tomorrow she can't even comprehend.

She is many things —
beggar of treats,
task interrupter,
climber and shredder of curtains,
constant gardener of the litter box,
and sometimes,
a graceful (yet somewhat vulgar) ballerina,
foot poised high above her head,
exposing herself to polite company.

But in this moment, she is the master
and I am the student.
As if to make sure I am paying attention to the lesson,
she turns my way and fixes her eyes on mine.
Without speaking a word of my language,
her eyes tell me this:

Mine is the path of adoration.
Human, stop tormenting yourself.
Watch and learn the many ways in which
I cherish this sweet existence.

He Liked Pretty Things, so He Chose Her

Admire, but be mindful.
If your reasons are selfish,
there is killing in the choosing.
With damage done, regret means little.
You can't unpick a flower.

On Incandescence

You are not my sun.
That magnificent, magnetic hope
has yet to unfold
his fated face to mine.

Yet just as careless children grasp
at untethered things that fly and fascinate,
you cast your covetous net over me.
Consent is of no consequence to your illegitimate claim.

I am the hunted, haunted thing
crushed by greedy hands
and the egocentric dreams of others.
I don't dream of you.

All fervor and no compassion,
you pressure and provoke until I'm undone
with suggestions that I'm the one.
But you are not my sun.

That great star rises above the horizon,
but not where I lie, stolen and cold.
The things that beam in this temporary prison
are just as synthetic as your affection for me.

A fraud as big as an empty sky,
you tried to disguise what you deem the real prize.
Now I lie here stuck and smothered, sticky with your iniquity,
pin-split and dead-still.

For a moment, you pulled me
from my open field, but you have not won —

you are not my sun.
And I belong to no one.

The Goal

You always show up,
raw and frantic.
The storm beats on.
Still, you push through.
Blood-smeared and sweating,
recalling your dream,
you continue chanting:
Someday, I will soar.

Charger

When she was a toddler,
she looked at me as if I were a God.
Today, I am merely mortal,
sweat-stained and straining
to lift one end of various
heavy pieces of furniture.
I watch as my daughter, now grown,
prepares and decorates her new home.

When her belongings are settled
and the cord must be cut,
I climb into a rental car to travel
several hours away from her.
A company has provided a Dodge Charger
that is painted in a bright, midlife-crisis red.
It feels too fun and sporty a ride
for a woman transporting empty boxes
back to her empty nest.

I arrive home amidst
the crackle of neighborhood fireworks,
the spark and shimmer of celestial popcorn
hurled into the heavens by the handful.
My first Fourth of July on my own.
Her Independence Day.
My cats run panic-laps
around the house, and I cry —
not for fear of being alone,
but because when life shifts gears,
the mind plays tricks and only the bad things stick.
What about the night I laid my infant daughter

next to me in bed and fell asleep,
only to be awakened later by her screams because
she'd rolled over the edge and hit the floor?
What of her tear-streaked face and outstretched arms
each time I had to leave her at daycare
to go make a living for both of us?
What about all the times
I'd wished for her to be somewhere else,
just for a second, so I could gather my thoughts
or have a moment alone?
How many times did I fail her, embarrass her, disappoint her?

Why is it so hard to remember
that we're all building the boat as we sail it?
We are so quick to flog ourselves with our failures
when we should look back, with wonder, at how much we did right.

Finally, the patriotism and tears subside,
and I remember that I have the rental car until morning.
I go for a midnight drive,
windows down and hair wild with wind,
classic rock blasting on the radio.
I pretend that the Charger is mine,
that I don't live in a state of fear
day to day, paycheck to paycheck.

I speed down one curvaceous highway
after another, aware of these things:

In my rear view, previous generations of mothers and fathers
who faced a similar moment and questioned their adequacy.

A parade of parents past,
each of them echoing the same lament —
We tried our best. We did the best we could.

In my head, the solemn understanding
that you only get one chance
to experience each unique
lifetime event or chapter.

In my heart, the beautiful woman
who once called me Mommy,
who now calls me Mom,
who will, if I'm lucky, always call me friend.

In the windshield, headlights revealing
only the amount of road I need to see
in order to stay on course in this moment —
and somewhere, beyond that,
my new life.

Something

The three of us
were lined up at the window —
two felines on the sill,
and I, their human,
standing between them.
I whispered, *Look...the sky*
is doing something,
but I didn't need to tell the cats.
They were well aware before I was,
being perfectly in tune with
the glorious business of nature,
as all animals are.
And as the sun set, we marveled
at the live color motion picture,
the miracle created by
billowing cumulus clouds,
the curve, pitch, and spin of the planet,
and a fireball 92 million miles away.
No distraction was succumbed to,
no photo was taken for
sharing on social media,
no task was completed before dinner,
not a grain of litter was
scratched or scattered onto the floor.
We were emptied of any
desire to "have" or urge to "do" —
we were merely an attentive trio
taking in a moment,
soaking up the big something
before it slipped away.

Watching My Friend Die
For Tanya Henderson, 1961-2018

I

The crowd is thinning as our peers exit the party.
Each year, the number of
departed souls grows exponentially,
and so does the awareness
that our group has been here for quite a while
and our own curfews are fast approaching.
The fact is sobering and we can't ignore it anymore:
it won't be long before Death —
that ancient and typically unwelcome guest —
will tap each of us on the shoulder
and tell us it's our time to leave.
There had been whispers that you'd be going soon.
Doctors finally said a handful of weeks,
but their estimate turned out to be generous.
In the early morning hours just a few days later,
you slipped out in silence when no one was looking.

II

You and I met when we were
paired at the factory.
They put us on line number five,
Seventh Circle of Hell —
too hot, too fast, prone to mechanical hiccups.
I was the new girl and you had to help me.
We eyed each other suspiciously
before setting ourselves to work.
I made glorious mistakes and
repeatedly shut the machines down.
Red-faced and eyes rolling, you'd fix each problem

and mutter a few words under your breath.
You thought I was daft, and I felt you were harsh.
For several weeks, we did our time together
and only spoke when we absolutely had to.
Then one day, I leaned across the table
and offered you a Jolly Rancher.
Your excitement gave you away in an instant.
I had discovered your weakness
and a way to make a connection:
you love candy.

III

I come to visit you in the hospital again,
and on this occasion, I bring saltwater taffy.
You proceed to sample one of each color
with childish delight as I settle in next to your bed.
For over fifteen years, we've discussed every topic
from the trivial to the profound.
Today, the talk is small,
but we both know what's really being said.
"Is it still hot outside?" is code for:
Don't be sad. I've made peace with my death.
"Yes, but it might rain later" means:
I'll miss you. I don't know how to let you go.
While millions of people wear ribbons
and blather on about a race for the cure,
the villainous cells in your body
are racing the rise and fall of the sun —
and they are winning.
I am watching you die in slow motion
and you are telling jokes to break the tension.

I laugh for your benefit, but I want to scream.
I am furious at my uselessness
and the absurdity of it all.

IV

The pairing was made permanent
and number five became our home.
We lived there 12 hours a day
almost every day of every month,
year after year after year.
We both snuck in the contraband.
Sour or sweet, chewy or hard,
each piece of candy laid the path to deeper friendship.
We slowly learned the facts and feelings of each other.
Both of us were single mothers
who had made our own way in this life.
We had loved passionately and completely,
only to be forcibly separated
from several men we had cared for —
either by death or because of their inner demons.
It was our lot to handle
every bill, every chore, and every hardship
the same way we went to bed each night — alone.
Still, we agreed that this path was better
than a life of physical or financial ease
spent with the wrong person.
We soldiered on every day, knowing our worth
and loving our hard-earned freedom.
People often thought us cold,
but we simply had nothing false within us.

We didn't tolerate rudeness or injustice,
nor would we put on a show or offer any fluff,
and if we did offer a compliment or smile,
one could know that it actually meant something.
We were both wildly curious
about spirituality and the unknown,
we each possessed a wicked sense of humor,
and we were truly grateful for everything —
most of all, for our amazing children.
We had these things in common.
All this, and our never-ending love of sugar.

V

You didn't wish to be the point of focus,
not even when you knew the end was near.
There were no melodramatic messages
or shocking posts on social media
in a bid for pity or attention.
You were never one to imitate
brightly colored blooms
or tree leaves that flap about
begging for the eyes or the heartstrings.
Always graceful and modest,
you resonated instead with the roots —
braving the darkness,
doing your difficult work and good deeds in secret,
providing support and nourishment
for all that flourished as a result of your existence,
always digging ever deeper
to form the great anchor.

VI

We're in yet another hospital room
and it's the last time I will see you alive,
though I don't know that yet.
We've told our jokes and reminisced,
and I've caught you up on work-related news.
It's getting late and I know you are tired,
so I tell you I should probably head home.
I stand up and say, "I love you."
As I say it, I make it a point to maintain eye contact
for longer than I normally would.
This kind of intimacy is hard for someone
as used up and broken as I am,
and it feels like I'm wearing
an itchy sweater that I need to take off,
but I wear it.
I bend down and hug you.
Holding you close,
I can feel the tubes under your hospital gown
and hear the steady hiss of oxygen
being delivered to your nostrils.
I hold on for an extra moment
because I need you to know
how much you mean to me.
I keep holding on because I need you to feel
all the things that words cannot express.
This is the only thing I know to do.
This is how I walk to the edge of the plank with you.

VII

I won't pretend to know where you are now.
I can't even get a grip on this lifetime,
let alone understand another.
Just for a moment, allow me to believe
that the next world we inhabit will be
whatever magical place we envision.
As I drift off to sleep beneath
the dream catcher you gave me,
I imagine our reunion at a grand afterparty
on a soft, sandy beach beneath a starlit sky.
As I make my way along the ocean's edge,
I'll meander through a maze of
tiki torches, sandcastles, beach blankets, and bonfires.
And then, I'll hear it —
your loud and mischievous voice,
restored to its full, pre-cancer power.
I'll follow the sound
and find you at the refreshment table,
your arm buried elbow-deep in a giant bowl of candy.
I'll pour us some coffee and pull up two chairs.
With all the time in the universe and nowhere else to be,
we'll laugh about how we finally escaped number five
and marvel at the fact that something better
really had been waiting for us
all along.

Alive

It isn't enough to simply inhabit —
to suck up oxygen and take up space
while entangled in a safety net
of familiarity and status quo.
Comfort must be exchanged for growth.

It isn't useful to recoil from what terrifies —
the roller coaster ride, the cross-country flight,
the big audition, the high dive,
the first date, the possible mistake.
At least you learned.

Complacency could never breed
the satisfaction that only stems
from fears faced down and disquietude engaged.
The thrill is in the reaching.
The victory lies in the fact that you tried.

Failure can be measured
by each swell and ebb of the ocean's tides
that passes without strengthening
the spirit, body, or mind.
To remain unyielding is to die.

I'd rather go for broke,
crashing and burning a path to extremes.
Test me, bend me, let me be unnerved
so I don't gaze through ordinary eyes.
As I move among the walking dead, let me be alive.

I'm Leaving You for Reykjavík

We were on the phone discussing
the possibility of a shared vacation.
In a healthy relationship,
each person typically mentions
the place — or places — they dream of visiting,
then both parties come to an agreement,
or at least some kind of compromise.
I submitted the idea of Iceland.

Your response was to let me know
that my desired destination
was somehow wrong.
You didn't say, "That's interesting,
but I'd prefer to vacation someplace else."
You didn't say, "Next time, I'll take you there
if you come with me
to a country I choose this time."
No. You simply stated,
"You don't wanna go to Iceland.
Just go to England with me, instead."

While I have nothing against England,
what's frightening is that this
is not a rare occurrence —
your undermining me,
ignoring me, choosing for me,
like I'm some five-year-old girl who
doesn't know what she wants or needs,
as though my lifelong wishes
don't matter and never did.

You like action movies,

so that's all we ever see at the theater.
When we're in the car,
you take control of the radio
and we listen to your favorite tunes.
I'm constantly dragged to sporting events
even though you know I can't stand them.
What you want to eat always trumps
my choice when we dine out.
You like to jog, so now you expect me
to become a runner, just like you.
My requests for equality always fall on
deaf and self-centered ears, but

newsflash: I am not you.

And I've dated so many like you.
Sometimes they employ bullying tactics,
but sometimes they do it with
a smile, a hard-on, or a kiss —
after all, a spoonful of sugar
helps the life-control poison go down.
No matter how they do it, it's all the same —
it's cruel, it's unfair, it's domination.

"Just go to England with me, instead."

Instead...
Meaning
My dreams instead of your dreams.
Meaning
What I need instead of what you need.
Meaning

Me instead of we.
Meaning
Instead of listening to you, I will
immediately dismiss anything and everything
you hold dear without batting an eyelash,
like I did just now.
Meaning
Instead of letting you express yourself,
I fully expect you to vanish into a world
of my creation and desires.
Meaning
Instead of being difficult, just give in.
You may not like it, but you'll get used to it.

When I was a weaker woman —
when I loved myself less —
I would have smiled and surrendered.
I would have fake-laughed and let it go,
scared to offend or rock the boat,
but that's not me anymore.

I am done being polite.
I'm done with disappearing into
someone else's existence.
I will not lie on my deathbed and watch
my partner's life flash before my eyes.
I won't settle for not being represented in this union.
The last time I checked,
there were two people in this relationship.

Or, at least...there used to be.
I won't be meeting you for dinner tonight.

Nothing you have to offer could be
as satisfying as standing up for what I deserve,
and nothing could ever taste as sweet
as the freedom to be who I truly am...
except for, maybe, some traditional Icelandic food.
I just purchased a plane ticket.
I can almost taste the skyr and brennivín already.

Nature Documentary Nightmare

I

I'm only ten minutes into
an animal documentary,
and here I go again — I'm about to cry.
As a lion closes in on an antelope
and prepares to pounce,
I yell, *Don't you dare!*
But then, the camera cuts
to a pair of hungry lion cubs
who wait for their mother to return
with fresh antelope for breakfast,
and the thought of them starving
is equally unbearable.
Antelope, lion cubs, antelope, lion cubs...
I'm spinning into madness.
I just can't deal with the endless conundrum —
who should we root for?
If one must die so another can survive,
which being most deserves to live?
Don't we all wish for a long, painless life
and love our offspring beyond understanding?
Doesn't each fish, insect, and animal
value their life as much as we cherish our own?

II

I have always felt connected
to everything on Earth.
When I was a child, I once tried to lick
the top of my cat's head.
The results were unsatisfactory for us both,

but I'd only been trying to return her affection
and make her feel more loved.
I talked to small spiders
that camped out in the corners of my house,
and when one of them moved into my
old, broken flute case, I named her Vibrato.
When I learned that a large tree requires
up to 200 liters of water per day,
I went straight to the nearest wooded area,
plastic squirt guns in tow,
and I shot at every exposed root in sight.
I ran through the trees screaming,
Are you thirsty?? Are you getting enough to drink?!
I was the girl who was constantly coming unglued
because she loved this world so fiercely.

III

When my daughter was only five,
I saw many signs that she was prone
to my particular brand of suffering.
One day she looked up at me and said,
*It hurts to be someone who
cares about the world so much.*
I held her tight, aware of the
painful path that lay before her.
But how could one not care after
looking upon this glorious planet?
Isn't it better to spend your life
in bittersweet rapture, having your heart
broken wide open by compassion again and again,
rather than feeling nothing at all?

IV

The antelope did not survive.
She was sacrificed for the family of lions,
and my sorrow couldn't save her.
I know that I was not her keeper,
I can't prevent all suffering,
and always, in each moment that passes,
something must die.
I only have the power to fully appreciate
every living thing I meet,
and to say to them — either with or without words —
what we all hope someone will convey to us
before we stop breathing, and that is simply this:
I bear witness to your beauty.
I see you.
Your life matters.

Drinking with Ernest Hemingway

You were a drunkard, a womanizer,
and sometimes, an ungrateful brute.
Like Mozart and a select handful of greats,
you seemed a genius placed into the
body of a tyrannical infant.
Maybe that's the trade-off:
if you get to be one of the disproportionately talented,
perhaps you must be deficient in other ways.
There are many people who would sacrifice anything —
their possessions, their looks,
their good health, their virtue —
for the ability to create just one masterpiece.
Whatever the reason, sometimes the most
unrefined instrument is the one
that produces the most resonant sound.

Right now, I am sitting at an ancient desk
where you once sat and left your mark —
several circles left by your cup
because you were too thoughtless
or too deep in your cups to use a coaster.
It's 1 a.m., and I am pounding the bourbon with you,
thinking out loud, interviewing the dead.
Did you feel that you were chosen?
Did you know it was your mission
to spin sentences into gold?
Were the right words ready and waiting inside you?
Did they just rise to the surface easily,
like champagne bubbles, or was it agony,
having to sort and torture them out?
How did you do what you did?
Damn it, I want you to tell me your secrets.

The house moans about aging,
its boards creaking and joints popping,
but you are silent.

Let's face it — you could be such an ass,
you probably wouldn't answer me, anyway.
I am thumbing my nose at you,
but in the same breath, I must salute you.
Most of us will never be
a Hemingway, a Rembrandt, or a Mozart.
At best, if we are lucky, we might be a Salieri.
The mediocre masses will continue to travel
to places like this, where you or the
other masters worked and played.
We will admire the objects you used,
running our fingers over them if we are allowed,
knowing that this is the closest we will come,
while on this earth, to touching God.

So tonight, I raise my glass to you, Big Papa —
larger than life wordsmith,
Lord of the Other Rings.
A simple toast from this humble visitor,
just a soon-to-be old woman
who was dreaming about the literary lion.

Sometimes, Love Is Spelled O-C-D

My daughter was driving me across town and
telling me the story of the ill-mannered housemate,
the beast who'd broken one of her plates.
"He grabbed it from the microwave
with his bare hand," she explained,
"and was somehow surprised that it was hot,
even though he'd just heated it for several minutes."
She paused to give me a look that said,
Can you believe that crap?
"So, anyway, he dropped it on the floor and it shattered.
He didn't even apologize."

"How rude," I offered.
I knew what was coming next.

"I had four dinner plates, four salad plates,
four bowls, and two coffee cups as a set.
Now I have only three salad plates,
and I can't buy one separately.
What am I supposed to do with *three* salad plates?"

She sighed. I only had to wait a few seconds
before she spoke of her solution.

"I guess I'll just have to break two bowls,
two dinner plates, and one salad plate.
Then I'll have a matching set for two."

She stated this as though it was
the solitary bolt of common sense
that held together a universe
which was otherwise insane.

I sat back in the passenger's seat
and marveled at this creature.
Only I could listen to such proclamations
and find them endearing.
After all, she came from my body and
inherited some of my sensibility.

I had once stared into a mirror as a child,
closely examining my bottom row of teeth —
two of which refused to align with the others.
"Well," I'd whispered to the other Jenn in the glass,
"at least the crooked ones are exact opposites
and they both turned inward, toward each other,
making them all symmetrical. Otherwise,
I'd have to pull those troublemakers out."

So, I understand my daughter's dilemma.
Some things simply cannot stand.
Call us crazy, laugh if you must,
but you won't be invited to our dish-crashing party,
where this perfectly odd pair of ducks
will be busy doing God's work,
keeping the world balanced
and making things even.

Reckless Behavior

Why did I kill the gnat?
It was purely accidental,
that slaying by the river
where I sat attempting to write.
I had been squinting into a page
made too white by the sun,
when upon that brightness
the insect did alight.
I only meant to swat it away,
but I was careless with my swipe
and it smeared instead of taking flight.
Nothing left but a dainty blood painting,
delicate scarlet trail, world's smallest comet.
Does this tale have any purpose?
I like to think it might,
for here lies a chance to contemplate
all such seemingly miniscule crimes,
and to recognize that reckless thumbs
can be just as deadly as the knife.
Right now, you may be a relative giant,
godlike in your ability to easily
pardon or take each tiny life.
But show mercy when you can,
because the tables always turn
and one day, each of us will be the gnat.
Am I right?

Pandemic Full Moon
May 6th, 2020

Today, I was evicted from my home
by a surprise army of termites.
I woke up to find them on the nightstand,
on the bed covers, in my hair.
After several hours of using a spray gun
and vacuuming as I cried,
I was forced to retreat.
I no longer own a working car,
so I called a taxi and checked into
a cheap hotel in my own town —
an accidental tourist going nowhere fast.

Now, it is dark. I leave the hotel lobby
and walk the city streets looking for food,
but almost everything is closed.
I'm wearing a mask —
not the one I used to wear
when I would pretend to be okay,
but a new one.
We all wear them now.

I walk past an empty cigarette pack
and a dead kitten.
A car rolls by, too slowly,
full of men who honk the horn
and scream obscenities at me.
I don't know where I will get my next meal
or if I'll have enough money to pay for it.
I don't know what my chances are
if I get the virus, my lungs always having been
the weakest part of my body.
The world is all debt and doubt and death.

Still, I stop walking to stoop down
and pull off my mask so I can smell
a honeysuckle bush in the moonlight.
Still, there are always small pleasures
and treasures buried in the wreckage.
Still, the brief ride on this planet
is worth the price, however steep.
Still, for now, I am here.

A & W

But not the root beer brand.
Instead, two characters carved
into a coffee shop countertop,
slasher-movie-style letters
scratched into posterity
for any of the future caffeinated
who care to notice.

Andrew and Wendy?
Alison and Winston?
Anna and Winona?
It hardly matters.
Someone had someone else.
They had each other.

I do not add any initials
to this permanent wooden
display of partnership.
There is no letter to go with my J,
ampersand sandwiched in between.
All I bring to the table
is myself. *"But I am enough,"*
I think as I once again
carve that truth into my consciousness,
engrave it inside the walls of my heart.

To My Life Partner

I may never lay eyes on you.
In fact, it's possible that you don't exist,
because what they say isn't true —
there is not a shoe for every foot,
a sight for every sound.

No one is at fault.
A life alone is no more a punishment
than being struck by a Steinway that falls
from suspension ropes four stories above.
Things are simply meant to happen.
Or, they are not.

There is no bitterness.
I am prepared to paddle this canoe built for two
through this life, across the River Styx, and into eternity
by myself, if that is my fate.
I've been through worse.
As gracefully as I can,
I will handle it.

But if our paths should intersect,
it will be at the auspicious place
where superhuman patience meets
hard-won understanding.

I won't need to be familiar
with the flesh and bones of you.
I will know you by your essence.
You will be as respectful as your words,
as kind as your deeds,
as gentle as your touch.

You will know my recognition of you
by the look on my face.
It will be the expression worn only by
the truly grateful who have
too long gone without.

And I imagine that a similar look
illuminated the face of Helen Keller
as water poured into her outstretched hands
and her eyes widened at the world she could not see
because everything was suddenly clear.

One can't help but appear awestruck
as the everyday is made miraculous —
when suddenly, there is a name to pair with
an incredible thing that is felt,
and the meaningful connection is made at last.

A Bird's View

I gazed up into the
vast gray of a cloudy midday
and spotted a single hawk,
a booming airbus of a bird.
He was soaring, swaying, swooping —
just showing off really,
as he should.

But I marveled that, once again,
I was the only one who seemed to notice.
An entire town full of people
remained mostly oblivious
to the other city that bustled
just a few feet above —
endless sky and every treetop
full of creatures more gracious and graceful
than we will ever be.

As I watched,
the hawk dramatically dipped
as if issuing a dare:

Look up, you beings with
your ill-used brains and
trouble-making thumbs,
always numbly wreaking havoc
and missing the point.
In this universe of connection
and boundless beauty,
you choose to remain deaf and blind
to the staggering symphonic experience
that surrounds you.

*I challenge each of you to raise
your head and your awareness —
to notice, for once,
something other than yourself.*

A World Without Witches

"Mommy, is the witch with the knife gonna come back and kill us?"
— my daughter, after witnessing my rape and attack in 2001

You were just short of four years old
and watching a cartoon on a lazy afternoon
when a stranger came crashing into our apartment.
When he wrestled me onto the bed
I knew what was about to happen,
but I wasn't concerned for myself.
I only wanted you free of danger,
so I yelled and told you to run —
run outside, run far away,
run to find an adult you knew you could trust —
but you wouldn't leave.
Like a soldier who remains on the battleground
with a wounded comrade until the very end,
you would not abandon me.

You had gone from watching "The Care Bears"
to witnessing live pornographic violence
within the space of a few seconds.
Born under the sign of Leo,
you were not some delicate pig-tailed flower,
but already a lioness,
roaring, fighting, staying,
bravely facing what many will never see
and what most people couldn't handle,
before you could even write in cursive,
ride a bicycle, or tie your shoes.
You didn't understand it,
you couldn't make it stop, but you
refused to let me suffer alone.
You held that horrific space with me,
crying, staying.

What did you learn that day?
That safety is not a given.
That at any moment, terror can come
screaming into your life like
a nightmare freight train gone off the tracks,
headed straight in your direction.
That your mother is not a superhero,
like you previously thought.

It's true, I can't always protect you —
not then, under our own roof in the middle of the day,
and certainly not as you move farther away,
growing independent from me, as you should.
I wish I could promise you
a world without witches or monsters —
the kind who control, assault, and degrade,
the ones who view the planet
as an all-you-can-hurt buffet
and help themselves to what is not theirs to have.

Yes, evil does exist,
but never become so cynical that
you close yourself off and lock your heart away —
that's only a different, slower way to die.
We survived, but not for you to
just exist in paranoia or bitterness.
I want you to expand, dance, hunger, radiate, feel,
dream, persist, dare, ROAR.

And if there comes a day
when I can't be with you anymore,

if you fear or doubt,
if you begin to feel like
What's the point?...

go to the top of the nearest mountain.
Listen to the wind and the branches and the birds,
and let them remind you, again —

You are here to be dazzled by all of this.
You thrive when you share your gifts
and heal others with your beautiful, courageous heart.
You win by not allowing the wicked ones
to dampen your desire to live
or your love of this world.

Cheap-Ass, Broke-Down Department Store Houseplant

You weren't with the other plants
in the garden section, indoor or outdoor.
I found you in the Land of Misfit Items,
the random aisle where the
deeply discounted go to die.
The only synthesizing thing in sight,
stuck between cans of spray paint
and pore-refining face masks,
you were pushed to the very back of the shelf,
hidden like a dark family secret,
marked with an embarrassing,
bright-yellow sticker: *55 cents.*
It seems they tried everything to kill you,
short of pinning a "good luck" note
to one of your brown, shriveling leaves
and setting you down on the
broken white line of Interstate 30.

But your terrible beginning was deceptive,
because I stumbled upon you, and surprise —
you won the houseplant lottery.
No more flimsy plastic cup,
but a soft bed of organic soil
and a proud pot of earthen clay to cradle you.
No more drought, but a steady diet
of filtered water and top brand fertilizer.
Now, you have the best window-seat in the house
and classical music to keep you entertained
while I'm away at work.
Even in the fanciest home of the richest of the rich,
you wouldn't be treated better.

Would Bill Gates ask you how you're doing
first thing in the morning?
Probably not.
Would Oprah sing you a song at bedtime?
Doubt it.

I believe you do have a consciousness,
but how complex is it? Are you able to wonder
why I saved you, why I bestow such love and care
when everyone else had left you for dead?
I can only answer: this is just what I do.
I reach out to my fellow forgotten ones
to offer them more than they ever expected,
to gift them with happiness they didn't see coming.
I visit an elderly woman in town
who lights up and talks a mile a minute because
she's so excited to have someone listen.
I'm a regular at a local fast food joint because
I take donuts and books to the drive-thru cashier
who suffers from depression and chronic pain.
I feed all the homeless neighborhood kittens
and try to nurse the sick ones back to health.

It's not about pity, and I'm no saint.
I don't expect anything in return,
not from any plant, animal, human, or higher power.
For all my kindness, I still might die alone,
but it doesn't matter — I will die content.
It was enough to watch you
grow larger and greener each day,
to see you bend gratefully toward the sunlight
that you were almost denied forever.

What bliss, what a satisfying life
spent loving others with no agenda,
giving away hope with both hands,
and choosing those who otherwise
would have remained unchosen.

Social Media, Translated

Social media is largely a sea of insecurity,
a place where the masses
cast each status in search of validation,
fishing day and night for attention and compliments —
those common, meager substitutes
for love of one's self.

With that one joke, insult, overshare,
humblebrag, rant, or selfie too many,
we have all screamed into the endless swirling
whirlpools of cyber-yearning,
and no matter our method, mood, or language,
the message, at its heart, is always the same:
Please, someone...see that I am valuable.
Please, let me know that my existence matters.

And I used to be
the leader of this needy fleet,
my voice the most persistent and annoying
in my efforts to prove — both to others
and myself — that I had worth.

So now that you see
my online presence lessening,
why do you worry?
Be glad for me, as I'm no longer clinging
to a flimsy life raft built from likes.
After so much turmoil, I'm quietly and happily
sailing toward my true north,
a navigator seeking calmer waters,
captain of a steady ship.

All the Bikes in Denmark

I spent years slinging trays in a factory,
bending, lifting, sweating, racing,
working until my fingers blistered
and walking until my feet bled,
saving mere scraps and saying prayers —
all for a chance to stand here in this
Nordic place that's so famously happy.
All that, to roam the land of Legos
and walk amongst the descendants of Vikings
while eating superior pastries and weaving
through all the bikes in Denmark.

I've wandered historic streets for days
and marveled at Danish customs and delights.
Now, I stand alone in a harbor
at a very late hour on a September night.
The stars are blazing, the world is quiet,
and all the bikes in Denmark are at rest —
leaning against each other like drunkards,
propped up on kickstands in parking lots,
attached to their proper bicycle racks.
A stone fish-girl sits in the water close by,
but she looks away from me.
She doesn't care about my lifelong journey
to get to this moment, nor do any of the Danes,
but I whisper into the Copenhagen air:
"Look at what I've done."

And with those words, I don't simply mean
that I made my way from Arkansas poverty
to a stunning tourist city on another continent,

but that I shifted from a place of hopelessness
to a state of believing that I can perform
the most powerful kind of alchemy.
Yes, I turned hundreds of thousands of trays
into a magical trip and a realized dream.
But far greater, I have also turned
a trail of family destruction into an abandoned path,
the cruelty and violence of others into forgiveness,
the wreckage of abuse into tools of empathy and healing,
and my own staggering pain into creative gold.
Just think— if I can do all that,
what else might I be capable of?
The possibilities are more numerous
than all the bikes in Denmark.

Scandinavia

I was deep in a volcanic cave
on a piece of the planet that sometimes
seems forgotten by the sun.
It was the month of September,
but I shivered and saw my breath.
The tour guide glanced at his thermometer
and made the announcement
that confirmed my discomfort:
"32 degrees Fahrenheit."
In Celsius-speak, that's zero, bone-chilling,
the temperature that hardens.
That was inside the cave,
but conditions outside were not much better —
dense clouds, spitting rain, a temperature in the 40's.
This, I marveled, *is Scandinavian summer*.
And if this was summer, what the hell was winter like?
I'd been told that on some days,
there were only 3 to 4 hours of sunlight, arctic winds,
the type of cold that could threaten sanity.
Yet people choose to live in these countries,
and they are consistently reported to be
the most content people in the world.
Yes, they have astounding landscapes,
progressive ideas, concern for the greater good,
eco-friendly policies, and ABBA.
But upon reflection, I thought a key component
might actually be the climate.

Happiness comes easily enough
when the weather does most of the work for you,
when you're sitting on a tropical beach with an
alcohol-filled coconut in hand. But that type of happy

will always be fleeting, and it wouldn't feel pleasing
if you experienced it all the time
with no bitter chill to provide contrast.

In the Nordic lands, most of the year
is a struggle for comfort and well-being.
One must constantly create their own warmth —
not just by way of heat and shelter,
but with self-care, kind acts, quality time with loved ones,
and deep gratitude for the smallest of pleasures,
because without these things, it would all be too bleak.
The flame is a symbol of hope and
the candle is at the center of everything —
holidays, family meals, even placed in windows
to uphold tradition and serve as a reminder
for themselves and their neighbors...
Hold tight. There have been dark times,
but there are brighter days ahead.

Centuries of harsh conditions
have taught these people a secret:
true happiness is like a fire — you must tend to it.

I was more than 30 meters below the Earth's surface,
musing on these things while my teeth chattered,
when the guide said it was time
for the Darkness Ceremony.
"Turn off your flashlights!" he yelled.
When the last bulb was clicked off,
we stood for several minutes in silence,
and I experienced something that took my breath away.

This was not just darkness, but the total absence of light.
It felt like a *negative* amount of light,
if that's even possible,
as if all light had been sucked away and
we were collapsing into a black hole.
No vague outlines of shapes,
no way to see your own hand
right in front of your face,
no adjustment of sight.
The eyes desperately grab at the darkness
for something, anything,
only to find more darkness.
Disorientation sets in —
are you standing perfectly straight,
or are you leaning now?
Then, logical or not, the panic begins.
Nothing seems to exist anymore,
nothing but the blackness.
What if this is all there is now?
What if this lasted forever?

Just as I felt I might scream,
the tour guide said something I'll never forget:
"This is as dark as it gets."

As dark as it gets.
But is that true?
What if you said that to the holocaust victim,
the slave, the child abuse survivor,
the mother who lost all of her children?
How many humans have faced

what should be unbearable, yet persevered?

But perhaps nothing is more Scandinavian
than the human heart —
a precious, tiny territory of infinite resilience
at the center of each of us,
fighting to keep the flame of hope alive,
even when pelted with
cold and darkness unimaginable.

If you are still here, it's not the end.
Protect your light. Crawl out of your cave.
Lift your head up and wait for the sun,
knowing that everything in the universe
dips and spins and comes around again.
And if we gather our hearts together
to drive out the darkness,
this planet will experience
not only a wave of life-affirming light,
but an abundance of it.

The Mighty

The princess types have hands unworn.
No manual labor, no cuticles torn.
They painted and filed as I clawed to survive.
They make hateful comments and cast judging eyes
      upon these hands.

Hands that clenched as I was bruised
by those in the throes of the beer bottle blues.
They tried to save others who wailed in the night,
but being so little, it was a weak fight
      using these hands.

I struggled to build a life on my own
with only the unhealthy methods I'd known.
The dysfunctional handling of people and money
were all I'd been taught, so always left empty
      were these hands.

I used them in ways surreal and obscene
to prepare my rapist to violate me.
The knife in my ear told me to,
so I did what I had to do
      with these hands.

These hands,
subjected to a lifetime of lies
and unfair assumptions.

The rich saw my hands and said —
They are not adorned
with precious metals or gemstones.
They are rugged and plain.

We can tell she comes from poverty.
She must not be valuable.

Other women saw my hands and said —
They are small, unshapely, and scarred,
just like her body.
She isn't voluptuous,
or as smooth and unscathed as we are.
She must not be beautiful.

The men saw my hands and said —
They are tiny and defenseless.
She makes an easy target.
Taking her down will be simple.
She must not be strong.

But know this:
you should never underestimate
the things on this planet
that appear small or insignificant.

The cell is most often invisible to the naked eye,
yet it's the essential component,
the building block and bringer of life.

The atom is purely microscopic,
but when split, it is capable of leveling entire cities
and shifting the course of history forever.

And I'm not just some paltry, scuffed-up ornament,
but more like a supernova stuffed inside a locket.
This seemingly second-hand trinket of a body

can barely contain a miraculous power
that awaits its moment to burst forth
and transform the world.

These amazing, persevering hands
are forever linked in solidarity
with my kindred, who are known as:
the exploited, the forgotten, the neglected,
the unwanted, the downtrodden, and the abused.
I am proud to stand as a member
of this army of the rejected ones
who are still brave enough to attempt
to love themselves and the world around them,
despite an existence of terror and dishonor.

And each time you see our ragged palms
with fingers outstretched,
reaching for the respect we deserve
and offering our great gifts of
mercy, understanding, and resilience to all,
you would do well to remember
that you are gazing upon
the hands of The Mighty.

From Genesis to Revelation

I

It's a little-known fact
that the first words
Adam ever spoke to Eve were:

That was fun. but I just saw another woman
on the other side of the garden,
and I think I better like the looks of her.

This was the original sin,
which fertilized the eggs of
heartbreak and self-doubt.

Primordial woman, newly minted,
was already made to feel that despite her
novelty and perfection, she was not enough.

II

After we had flirted by phone for some time,
a man hinted that he would like
to know my measurements.

I texted the circumference of
each womanly swell and dip,
the all-too-important invisible rings
surrounding my heavenly body.

His response was simply:
Well, you're no Marilyn Monroe, that's for sure.

We had never spoken of the famous blonde before,
yet here she was, invading both our conversation and my mind.
Here I was, already being compared and not measuring up.

It was the first sign of his superficiality and callousness,
the first offense of many.
But that had never stopped me before.

III

In the garden of Eden, Eve died while choking
on a lump in her throat, but it wasn't a wedge of apple.
It was the initial stone of rejection.

IV

Even as a child, I subconsciously sought out
the cruelest male in the playground.
My crush was always the mini sadist,

the boy who sat in the grass
pulling the wings off some delicate insect,
simultaneously admiring and destroying it.

V

No star in the universe is any less resplendent
for having remained unseen
by human or telescopic eyes.

Stunning and miraculous,
both in life and during a cataclysmic firework death,
the majesty of each is absolute and requires no validation.

And I am no less spectacular
for having gone unloved or unappreciated
by another.

VI

Well, sir:
you're no knight in shining armor, that's for sure.
But it turns out, I never needed one.

VII

A magnificent star in a distant galaxy
explodes and begins its slow death,
and I step into my power.

I am not Eve. I am not Marilyn.
And I don't wish to be either of them.

…I am the goddess of my own garden.
(Where disrespect will never be tolerated again.)
This will be a space of integrity and kindness.
(A warm, safe place for self-acceptance to grow.)
From now into forever, I will stand solidly in my truth.
**(To love myself as I am
is my source of strength and my birthright.)**

And there was in the beginning, is now,
and ever shall be, worthiness without end.

(Amen.)

Tack så jättemycket — Swedish
Mange tak — Danish
Tusen takk — Norwegian
Þakka þér kærlega — Icelandic
Kiitos paljon — Finnish
Thank you so much — English

Let's start with teachers, because their influence on both individuals and communities cannot be overstated. In some cases — especially when a student feels lost and worthless — a teacher can actually save a life with their guidance and kindness. The following educators believed in me, inspired me, and kept me going when almost every part of me wanted to give up:

Ms. Bowser (4th grade), Mrs. Nash (5th grade), Lujuana Warner (grades 7 & 8), David Dickey (grades 7 & 8), George Pokorski / Mr. "G" (grades 7-9), Rick Hammer (grades 10-12), David Rollins (college, HSU), Mitzi Bass (HSU), Tom Chase (HSU), David Etienne (HSU), Andy Anders (college, ATU), Karen Futterer (ATU), and Tommy Mumert (ATU). You all helped me — more than you'll ever know. The biggest THANK YOU to each of you.

Sandra Rowe is the person who set me on the path to living a more moderate, healthy, and fulfilling life. She introduced me to the books and teachings of Pia Mellody, a world-renowned lecturer on codependency and the emotional dysfunction that stems from childhood trauma. Sandra also recommended The Green Shoe Foundation (www.greenshoe.org), where I took part in a week-long intensive group therapy program that both deepened my understanding of the effects of trauma and furthered my healing. I've spent time with several mental health professionals over the years, but without Sandra and the resources she made available to me, I'd still be swirling in a cesspool of self-sabotage and shame. I was incredibly fortunate to have her as my counselor (before she retired), and now I'm honored to call her my friend. Thank you, Sandra, for altering the course of my life for the better.

Thank you, Greg, for being a good and loving father to our Lana. You and I went through a lot together, and I know it was hard for you to watch me struggle to "grow up" (way too late, and without knowing how). The worst thing about abuse is that it doesn't just hurt the initial victim — like ripples on disturbed pond water, the painful effects spread and touch all people who get close to the wounded person at the point of direct impact. It took a long time for me to seek the help I needed, and I thank you for your patience with me. I'm glad we're still friends, and I'll always be rooting for you.

To the owners, baristas, and crew of Coffee Records — your coffee is the best around, your food is phenomenal, and your service is always friendly. Coffee Records is my favorite local hangout, and it's also where I wrote and/or edited several of the poems in this collection. Thank you for providing a safe, clean, and welcoming space where I can relax and create. Life is so much better since you opened for business, and our town is lucky to have you.

"Green" — my beloved, long-time friend...I am so thankful for you. We met at Henderson State University in 1994, and for over three decades, you've been nothing but generous and supportive. You were the first person — many years ago — to take me to an open mic poetry event. It reignited my passion for the art form, and played a major part in leading me to this moment, when I would finally have my own collection of poems to share with the world. I know I've been saying that the book is "almost done" for years, and I'm sure most people lost faith in me. But YOU always believed...and look, Green — I did it!

I'll be eternally grateful to a young man I met on a bus when I was just 14 years old. He was a new student in our school, from a country called Denmark — a place I'd never heard of. After a trip to the library to check out several books (no internet back in those days) and many hours of study, I was fascinated by his homeland, and other Nordic territories, as well. That fascination only grew over the years, and it eventually led me to visit several Scandinavian countries. Those visits led to the Scandi metaphors and themes that kept coming up in my poetry, and those themes became an integral and cohesive thread that runs through this collection. Life is funny, and you never know the impact you might have on another person's life, even when you're completely unaware. This book literally would not exist if I hadn't met that Danish student when I was a young girl. If he should happen to read this one day, all I can say is: Tak, for evigt.

To Aaron and Stephanie — I might have been born first, but you two have always seemed older and wiser than your years on this planet. You've both grown into such strong and compassionate individuals, and I'm constantly amazed by you. We are bonded forever — not just by blood, but more so because of our unique shared experiences and the way we've supported each other along the way. I will never stop hoping that you'll be showered with blessings and good luck, now and for the rest of your lives, because that is what you both deserve. Thank you for being the kindest and coolest siblings anyone could have.

And precious Lana...what can I even say to the human I love most in the world, when words could never be enough? You motivated me to heal and improve myself, and made me want to become the best mother I could possibly be. What an honor — what a privilege in this lifetime! — to be *your* mom. Thank you, for just being YOU. Don't let anyone shame or bully you for being yourself, and don't let anyone disrespect or abuse you, ever. You are already kind to all living things, but never forget to be kind to yourself, as well. I have always tried to let you know how special you are and how much you mean to me, and I will continue to do this for the rest of my days. Never, NEVER forget how unique and valuable you are as a person, or how much I love you...

About the Author

Jenn Howe is a poet, filmmaker, and photographer who currently lives in central Arkansas. Most authors use this space to list their educational and professional achievements, and while that's all well and good, Jenn wishes to utilize this space to let you know something much more important about her. She finally realized that worldly accomplishments and awards are fine, so long as you don't rely on them to provide your sense of self-worth. External glory — or lack thereof — does not define you, and you are worthy already, just because you were born. What matters is this: Jenn reached out for help in dealing with the aftermath of trauma and abuse, and so can you. She has learned how to live a much more functional, balanced, and fulfilling life, and so can you. She now lives authentically and holds herself in warm regard while deeply appreciating her experience on this beautiful planet, and yes...you can, too.

www.ingramcontent.com/pod-product-compliance
Lightning Source LLC
Chambersburg PA
CBHW030943090426
42737CB00007B/520